Home is Where I Hang My Pot

Poems and songs, fierce and gentle, from somewhere over the hill

Flloyd Kennedy

LIVERPOOL

Flloyd Kennedy

11 Heathcote Close

Liverpool, L7 6QA, Merseyside, UK

www.flloydkennedy.com

@flloydwith2ells

https://www.facebook.com/flloyd.kennedy

https://flloydwith2ells.bandcamp.com/
Book Layout © 2017 BookDesignTemplates.com
Cover Image © Terry Cripps 2020 - www.169.org.uk

Home is Where I Hang My Pot/ Flloyd Kennedy. -- 1st ed.
ISBN 978-1-8381946-0-4

Dedication

To the poets and singer-songwriters of Liverpool and the North West of England who've welcomed me to their Open Mics and encouraged me to perform and to publish my work.

Contents

Preface

Hey everybody, what's it like—
running up that hill of life,
tumbling over tufts of lichen,
finding it's ok to stumble,
fall to rise and fall again?
Doesn't matter that you bumble
straying from the path you chose,
all the proud and all the humble
rich or poor, weak or strong,
there is only one direction
and it's neither right nor wrong.
Life's an uphill journey for as long
as you can keep on going
striving with every fibre of your being
to reach the top, then you can stop. Except...

You never know you've reached the top,
not until you've past it.
You never know you've gained a skill,
not until you've mastered it.
You rarely value what you've got
unless you're willing to cast it
over your shoulder
where someone else can grasp it.
Hey! it's all a game of tag,
a tug of war with all the new stuff;

some for you, but what's for me?
Can I be the thing I want to be?

Wrong Question!

Can I make a go of being the thing I want to be?
Better...

If you're anything like me,
you always knew the answer
but didn't dare to put it to the test.
If I couldn't be the best
I wouldn't even chance it.
I'd dance around it,
stoking the fire,
thinking I was different,
but in fact I was just like all the rest–
maybe a better liar–
playing safe, settling for less.
Oh how depressing...

I confess, I have thought these thoughts
from time to time.
And probably will again.
But I don't think they define me,
or my life,
which has definitely had its moments.
          And now, on with the show.

viii

And still I grow

I am a Fractal.
I grow, and I divide.
I am an Algorithm
infinitely reflecting
infinite refractions.

I am a triangle
holding up the ceiling.
The ceiling is holding up the roof.
The roof is holding up the sky.
The sky is holding up the universe.

How strong is the sky
to hold up the universe!
The universe holds up
the power of Maths
to describe
the complexity of the world—

But Maths is exclusive,
a language I have never learned
beyond its tantalising edges.
Is there another way?
A process that can
provide the key
to understanding how, and if?
And if not, why not?

Is there a loosely structured system
to decipher and describe
the mysteries of life
one complex layer at a time?
A language free from dogma,
free from the bonds of certainty,
that yet adheres to
the constraints of
probability
while maintaining at its heart
at least the illusion of
functionality?

I do believe there is.
I call it
Art.

Home is where I hang my pot

Home is where I hang my pot—plant.
It happens that I move a lot,
from house to house,
from town to town.
I'm either leaving or arriving
on plot or a spot of land
where I make my stand
and I get on with surviving.

Coz whether there's work
or whether there's not,
I always have to have a pot.
It could be hanging by the window
or standing on the landing—
at first there's just the one
but pretty soon they'll come in pairs.
Their greeniness and spikiness
will slowly transform
into cascades of colour as
a room becomes a home
and my home becomes theirs.

I talk to my plants,
'not a little, but a lot.'
They respond with little waves
if there's a breeze, and if not
they just sit there,
being lovingly themselves—

not demanding, but expecting
to be tended, to be fed,
to be watered, and dead-headed,
to be left in peace to grow.
And how they grow. Triffid like
expanding into nooks and crannies.
High on cupboard tops they'll flow,
trailing their tendrils, and they'll glow
with life apparently unending.

I don't abandon them
when I hear the call to move along,
shift my aging carcass,
get away, write another song
in another town.
I put them down
for adoption, find loving families
to take them in. The stayers, the settlers
who don't just meanly hang a pot plant,
love it and move on.
No! They plant them in the garden,
shove their roots deep down into the soil,
leave them there, to toil their lives away
while sun and rain replace
my watering and talking regime.

Truth to tell, It gets me down
now and then, all this shifting,
changing, rearranging.

All the pots I've left behind—
they sustained me in their time,
nourished me while I maintained
my transient life style,
rife with motion,
keeping strife at bay
by moving on.

Not going back
but going on—
going on because it's
what I've always done.
I never run away.
You can't escape your troubles,
they'll follow you and find you,
jump up from behind you:
"Hey old friend" they'll say
"Fancy meeting you today.
Here we are together,
how happy can you be?"

So I stay put
until that day comes when
I know it's just not working out.
It's not you, it's me
(that's true for places
just as much as people)
and the way ahead
reveals a steeper curve,

a downhill swerve towards uncertain
yet familiar futures.

> *Give me a space to call my own,*
>
> *call it yours, but leave me alone.*
>
> *I'll plant my desires, and*
>
> *when they're full grown*
>
> *let me be the one to reap them.*

A place is found, an empty space
resounding hollowly,
un-curtained and unnervingly welcoming.
I'll unpack my curiosities,
fill my new life with activities,
with usefulness, with local delicacies.

It's never long before I spot
the vacant window-sill
where the sunlight can play
and dance upon the plants
I'll place with care
and love, and then I'll dare
to start again–
romancing the stone-ware,
plastic or ceramic pots
that hold the breath of new life,
photosynthesizing time itself,
creating space
for this old rambling rover.

I'll take cover.
Keep the window open,
just a tad.
Keep an eye on those buds,
fresh shoots, sprouting leaves,
the glowing colours, floral tributes to my
feeble attempts at normality.
My formless wanderings
take shape again within
the growing, ever changing, and yes,
sometimes dying flora of my life.
And I am home.

And still you grow.

Tiny spider plant,
a gift, gently snipped from
your mother's outstretched arm,
hastily wrapped in wet cotton wool,
popped into a poly bag, and transported
back to Liverpool in my backpack.

Modestly at first, nestling into the
company of a kindly Kalanchoe,
you reached downwards, roots
thickening, searching for the dark brown
safety of soil.

Slowly, your lime and jade striped points
sloped their length upwards, seeking sun;
sensing the power of meagre light through
dark winter days.

Greedily, you guzzled the water soaking
sweetly past your spikey leaves.
Insidiously, their tips inched higher,
wider, subtly spreading into the space
conceded by your florid friend.

Suddenly, one solo spike, thin and reed-like,
secreted shyly among the foliage,

escaped its hiding place, a scape
whose inflorescence dandles
miniature plantlets, inspiring each other
to softly flutter into the spring warmth.

Mightily, you embark upon motherhood,
bearing your babies with bravado
as the earth turns, and life yearns
to repeat itself, freshening the air
I breathe, a gift indeed,

And still you grow.

The ending is where it begins

First things first.
I'm going to start at the end
while there's still time.
Whatever that is.

There is always a beginning, a middle, an end,
My ending is beginning to bend around me.
It happens when you lose your mother.
Your boundaries become detached.
Unlatched memories drift
through space and time
like matchless galaxies shifting,
disturbing the fabric of your
remembered life.
Your beginning darkly
matters more and more,
and lest the middle of your life
should contract
into a white dwarf
of total insignificance,
you find yourself reflecting,
backwards,
into a hall of infinite mirrors
wherein lies – nothing.
No answers,
No questions.
No time to ask more questions.

You cannot even
conceive of what questions you might ask
because she is not there to answer them.
Especially not there to retrieve
answers from the black hole
into which disappeared all the questions she
refused to answer before she left.
While there was still time.

So, let's get straight to the end.
At least, how I would like it to be.

Not alone.
When the time comes,
please don't let me die alone.
If a tiny meteor plummets
into a sunlit sky,
invisibly indivisible
in its brightness
from all those particles of light
competing for attention,
did it ever happen?

But then again—why not?
What difference would it make?
There's nothing anyone can do,
there's nothing
I can do at that point.
Ah. But that's the very point.

It's not about the end,
the instant when existence ceases,
when the body is released from
the weight of present and consistent
Being-ness.
Is it? No!
It's more about
the bit before, the moments
of terrifying anticipation
when you lie there, spiraling
towards the harsh reality
of an insignificant
crash landing, wondering
what the hell was that about?

That's when you need
another body in the room,
banging on about
dreadful politicians,
and how humanity is going to
hell in a handbasket,
so you get pissed off
because you asked for it!
You asked for life.
You fought to grasp it,
long and lasting,
and now you just want it,
as your mother did,
all to be done and dusted.

Which is pretty much how I feel
most of the time,
even though time—as such—
does not exist.

Don't worry,
I'm not about to top myself
(or am I?)
I am determined,
as my mother was,
to see the whole thing through.

There was a time, back in the days
when I believed in time,
when I confused time with life itself,
thinking it was a mountain
waiting patiently to be climbed
and from whose peak
I'd claim the world as mine.
And I would shine my light
across the valley on the other side,
illuminating all the nooks and crannies
left in the dark by lesser mortals.

And I would have done it, too,
if only I could have found
a winch,
or a cable car
to get me up among the stars.

None of that 'one step at a time' nonsense,
I jumped, I leapt, I bounced,
I found myself
back where I began
time after non-existent,
paradoxical time.

Until suddenly,
without any apparent warning,
I find myself here,
and now,
on the other side of the living mountain,
wondering how I got here,
why the mystical promise
of the Road Less Travelled
winding mysteriously out of sight
turned into the road to
nowhere in particular.
The road to later,
and still later,
and please—

May I start again?

Mother of sons

She always wanted a son.
No!
I tell a lie. She wanted six sons.
Six tall strong sons who would love her
          and her cooking;
who would have to duck
their tall heads as they wandered
into her tiny kitchen,
who would pat her on her
short head from their great height
and duck away,
laughing,
          from her sharp tongue
as she remonstrated with them
for their impressive tallness.
Then they'd turn back
          and hug her.
And she would raise them to be kind
and to follow their passions, and
they would leave and
          they would return
with tales of great learning.
They would bring her
girls who would become
women of great passion and learning.
 And they would all
          love her cooking.

All this she dreamed
as she was growing up herself;
learning to keep her passions hidden—
learning that to love was to be hurt—
learning what she failed to realise
at the time was great learning.
          And also
learning that she was a terrible cook.
But that didn't stop her from learning
          how to be a better one.

And so, in time, with the help of
many cook books,
          and a long-suffering husband,
she began to create curries, roast meals,
scones her Scots mother-in-law
          would be proud of.

And then, a son.
He was a smiler.
Blue-eyes and golden hair,
from birth he was a
genial, likeable little chap.
Early to walk, early to talk–
didn't much like hugs.
          but he liked her cooking.

Soon after, a second son—a gazer.
Blue eyes, bronze hair.

Long hours in his little chair
he'd gaze into the distance.
Sometimes turning to catch her eye–
and smile—and turn away
        to gaze some more.
Hugs he would tolerate, at first.
        and he liked her cooking.

And so they grew, and like all children
sometimes they were kind,
        other times—were ghastly.
They took turns at being naughty because
though close in years
they didn't play together,
didn't have the same tastes at all.
        But they both like her cooking.

In time, they grew into tall, strong men,
kind and passionate—
        especially about learning.
They brought her girls who became
women of great passion and learning,
        who loved her cooking.

She grew up herself, just a bit.
Sometimes waiting for them to come by—
mostly getting on with her other passions,
        occasionally cooking.

From dreams of six sons
to the reality of two
some reductions
          don't bear quantifying.
They never duck their heads to
enter her kitchen
because she doesn't live in a
          tiny croft cottage.
They never pat her on the head
because they never learnt to
          patronise women.
They never stop by unannounced
because their partners have
          mothers of their own.
They never stop by, because they have—
as she encouraged them to have—
          lives of their own.

They never jump behind to grab her
in a bear hug.

Whatever...

          they still love her cooking.

Mother and daughter

Poem for 2 voices, (from the play "One Point Five" commisioned by The Wicked Ladies, Glasgow 1989, and revised as "Blame it On Your Mother", for Les Girls, Toowoomba 2003)

I always wanted a daughter.
There is something very special about a girl.
Boys are great—demanding—and great fun,
but a girl is something of your own.

I'll never forget the moment I first saw you
Long and slim, slimy, and so angry!
They placed you on my sagging stomach,
and you said:
"No!

"I want to be high up,
up in the clouds.
If I must be out here, I want to be
The One On Top." You were so special.
No other baby in the world had your cheek.
You learned so quickly, and you had so much
love to give.
[Love to give.]

I never minded waking up
at five am to feed you.
When I reached your crib
you'd be looking up and laughing,
longing to get stuck in to Life.

We'd dress you in the prettiest things—
your daddy was so proud of you.
[Daddy was so proud]. He would have given up
his beer money to dress you if I'd asked him.
[Ask him.] I couldn't, of course.
Couldn't—ask—for anything,
just had to wait and see what he'd give me.
And bright! The questions you would ask!
"Why is the moon bigger than the stars?
Why is cabbage green?
What do dogs dream about?"
Oh! I tried to answer as best
I could. I swore I never would
lie to you. [Lie to me!]
But when the only answer could be
"I don't know".
[I don't know—I don't know!]
you were so frustrated,
as if I should know everything in the world.
As if I could know everything in the world.
[As if I could].

I gave you all the knowledge I had.
I wanted you to know what I knew. Not to
make the same mistakes that I had made.
I knew you'd make your own
[my own]
make your own way.
[My own way].

22

I wanted to save you wasting time, wasting
one precious moment of your precious life.
Why start from scratch,
when I could help you start
from where I'd left off? Such a waste.

But no. [Oh no!]
You had to do it your way.
And your way was so like
my way. [My own way] Not the same,
but so like me. [So like me]
Even to the extent of cutting me off
the way I'd cut my mother off.
I thought that's what she wanted so
I cut [cut] her [her] free.
[Free!]

Talk about apron strings! It's not
apron strings that tie us together,
it's much more basic than that.
They placed you on my tummy
while the afterbirth was delivered.
I held you, touched you,
smelt you, knew you
before the cord was cut.
For me, it never was cut.
For me, you have never ceased to be
        part of
                my body.

Crying to order

I think I was dreaming.

I woke up, and looked at you
and for an instant you were dead.
Then my mind switched on,
knew it would miss you,
the children needed you
and anyway I had chosen you
and no-one else wanted me.
And although I can always cope with anything
I didn't want to cope without you.
Which was just as well
because you weren't dead.

 But then, neither was the dream.

The dream fills me with such
feelings of indescribable beauty
of promise and threatening tears.
It is the tears that give the dream away,
For I do not weep in reality.
At least, not often.
Never in public.
Sometimes I cry with rage or frustration,
tension contorting my body
as tears flow in the dark, in silence.

I cried so rarely as a child
that I would rush to a mirror
to see whether my face had changed
for no-one ever seemed to notice
that I was crying.
It seemed to me that it didn't.
My eyes were reddened.
I could have had a cold.

If anyone ever asked me if I was crying
I said I had a cold. They always believed me.
When my father died I cried quite a lot.
I said I had a cold. They believed me.
A fellow student found out—
"You're an odd one," she said, not unkindly.
"Your father died, and you never cried.
Why?"
So I did.

It is the only time I have ever cried to order.

Some nonsense rhymes

On a summer's day in the month of May
a man was gaily singing.
He tipped his hat and he fell down flat
while his horse went highland flinging.
His wife was nearly six foot two,
she couldn't bake for cryin'.
And his kids thought school was just for fool-
in' round, and not for tryin'.

Yet once upon a moonbeam
I sat and sang a tear.
A lamppost kept me company
and breezes came to hear.
The lamppost played the melody
till children filled the air;
discordant was our harmony
of rapture and despair.

Union calypso

My boss said to me the other day
"If you give up your union then I will pay
one thousand pounds if you don't strike no more".
I said "Strike me dead! Well, I'm not sure...

"If you can give me one thousand pounds
and all of my workmates that are around,
why can't you give me a rise in pay
then I won't need to strike any other day?"

Sporty calypso

In the summer of 1974
I'm feeling fit and ready to score,
so I put on my shorts and my new string vest
and run all the way to Budapest.

The man at the border say, "you come the wrong way,
the Olympic Games are in LA".
I thank him politely, but I say, "No thanks!
Los Angeles is full of goddamn Yanks."

A limerick

Two children born to one mother
grew up never knowing each other.
Though their beds were adjacent
the rivalry nascent
ensured sibling love undiscovered.

Where there's growth

Halfway to ecstasy

I'm halfway to ecstasy.
The road I tread is leading me
unsteadily towards a shore
where waves are pounding,
breaking down
the rocks of misadventure,
and there's more than one way
to crack a heart wide open.

Who needs drugs?
I did this to myself.
I pulled the zipper,
loosed the buttons
tore apart the wrapping,
found the core,
exposed myself.
It was fine, for a while.
Everyone enjoyed the show.
Then I tried to close the gap over the wound,
replace the protective shield.
But I lost the key,
broke the toggle, tore the skin.
The heart stays open
pumping glorious red raw vital life blood
to the sky. Nerve ends jitter,
shoot their glittering neurons round each other—
a spectacle to match the last days of a Galaxy.

Halfway back from ecstasy
casual thoughts and cool encounters
quieten the soul.
This double-pulsing paced Iambic plod
has pulled me back to now,
and I am—
present.
The universe spins so softly
you hardly know it's there.
Before I know it
I'll be ahead of myself again
thundering towards that rocky shore
where felt findings
pound themselves
to starry brightness.
And there's more than one way
to heal a heart.

This day (the sequel)

I knew this day would come.
I'm glad it took its time.
The days before were fine,
light, bright, tight
with unspoken promise.
When the gaps appeared
they just let in more light,
life seemed to glow
and time seemed to blow
warm dreams between the cracks.

I know this day will go. First though,
it will bring in its regiments,
battalions of dawning followers
adding weight to its already laden
boundless burden of grey
grains of doom,
that gather to form
nuggets of deadly nihilism.

In the days between
I hold the flighty beams
lightly, dancing with them,
flicking their ribbons around my body
revelling in reflected sparkles.
Every thought a probable idea,
each idea a possible project.

It has to be.
The sheer weight of my
manic dreaming has to give way to
something more mundane.
And so
the cracks grow wider.

This day is not new.
We are old companions.
We have travelled together—
long sea journeys to islands
overrun with strangeness
and the expert ignorance
of strangers.
We have slept in unsettling
discomfort, dozing
and drowsily avoiding
each other, in a tangle of
blanketed isolation.

This day cannot be ignored.
It cannot be discarded, or shunned.
I will wear it, bear it around my being,
strutting through a veil of torn dreams
while searching for the darning needle.
I will find that needle, sharp underfoot.
I will staunch the flow
of bloody tearing flesh
with gobbets of un-cried tears.

This day will go.
There will be light
at the end of the funnel
when ideas will flow again.
Some of them will even
take shape.
They'll spark and flicker into life
with heat enough to reveal
the next idea.
The days between will buoy me through
and over the horizon;
long enough to prove
that this day
will come again.

Awake

(a rap)

Are you awake?
When you got out of bed
what's the first thing you did?
Did you take time to think
about the day to come?
Or the one just gone?
Did you put the kettle on?
Look out the window,
basking in the flow of cars
and birds and people
taking the day to task?

Or did you pick up your phone
to check on Facebook,
to see if someone knew
you were alive?
Perhaps you checked for messages?
Perhaps someone had messaged back
but you were sleeping at the time
and so you missed it.
What a bind.
What a chat you could have had,
in the middle of the night
sharing stories and ideas,
making plans to catch a random flight
to Berlin, or Algiers.

As if.

Has the kettle boiled?
Make the tea, and think of something else
before you turn to Facebook
where you know there are hundreds
of people that you don't, or barely know.
'Coz if you resist the urge to look,
you can't deny the fact that—
if you were on your own before
you'll still be on your own.
Although it seems as though you've
friends galore, it's an illusion.
Like actors in a drama, screen or stage,
they're not expressing their own rage,
their confusions, or their passions—
it's an illusion.
If it's any good, it's a good illusion.

Are you awake now?
Or are you still in that dream state
wandering through alleyways of
other people's ways and means.
You may be moved by the shared
sorrows and their joys
when they start a new relationship,
make new work, get new toys.
They touch your heart
but they'll never touch your hand.

They'll never stand in your kitchen
while you make a cup of tea
They won't invite you to their homes.
They won't meet you at the airport
as you're passing through
They might arrange to come and visit you
when they come to your town
then they'll cancel
when something more important
comes around.
They're just another 'quote friend',
just another Facebook Friend,
a Find-a-Friend Friend,
another Friending friend.
Perhaps a Trending Friend?

Nah.

Are you awake now?
Or just 'woke'?

Are you so busy being well-informed
that you failed to hear the call
when the one who spoke out
needed help?
Were you listening?
Were you a good friend?
In deed?
Get a grip, woman.

This big bad world's inviting you
each morning,
to be the main attraction
in your actual life,
the life that's inciting you
to be as exciting as the ones you
fantasise about,
to take a chance
to blindly jump into the deep end
on your own, not waiting to be pushed
nor afraid of losing out.
Are you really awake?
To lost opportunities? To disappointment?
To frustration? To regret?
These are not negations—
these are indications,
proofs that you have cared,
that you have shared in the great
adventure of life, that you have given
more than you got. And why not?
Don't stop doing that. Dig your heart
out of the zombie land that
glows in your hand.
Look out of the window, start again.
Wake up to wonder—
to wonder what might come next.
And give it your best shot.

You need to be truly awake for that.

Her greatest fear

You're so brave! they say,
every time I jump
out of the bland
into the bold new
shiny adventure
that promises
it will all be different
somewhere else.

Me, Brave? No!
That's not how it goes.
Bravery means
risking everything
for someone else,
for the sanctity of life,
not for the thrill:

to save a puppy up a tree
or a kitten down a drain,
not to be seen
and not for gain;
or standing out
before the throng
affirming loudly
"might is wrong"
for if you don't
who will?

Now then!

If someone held me tightly—
tried to stopped me
from lightly flitting
out of the bland, the safe,
The place of
I-gave-it-my-best-shot,
the place of
too-hard-to-make-it-work-here,
I-need-to-move-on.
Oh look!
Over there looks good.
Bye!

That would be brave.
To risk the pain
I could inflict
dramatically resisting.
That selfless act
could save me
from myself,
forcing me to turn
to face the fear
that I pretend
does not exist,
the fear that—
I am
where bland lives.

I move on into the wide blue yonder
not because I'm brave
but because I'm afraid;
I'm drawn, not to danger
but to the glitter of potential,
just beyond my reach;
its enticing sparkles
concealing the essential fact
that it's really always just the same, only
Somewhere Else.
And by the time I realise that,
the fear has been subsumed so deeply
no one recognises it—
least of all me.

Me brave? No!
That's not how it goes.
Bravery is taking a chance,
putting your life on the line
to save someone else, friend or stranger
from imminent danger or pain.

Taking a chance on your own behalf
For the sake of a laugh, or financial gain
or avoidance of boredom, attempting to live
with more colour, less strife—
that's not bravery.

That's just life.

Volume control

The volume control is faulty.
Full throated child—hushed —is numb.
Sound flows, is heard,
resounds and feeling returns.
Listen: hear! More sound,
more feeling.
The sounding board
at rest
is silent,
not hushed.

And so, life
goes on...

I am my voice

(from "The Fall of June Bloom (or what you will)" by Flloyd Kennedy with William Shakespeare, produced by Thunder's Mouth Theatre, Brisbane, 2010)

I am not mad. I am my voice.
Where my voice is, I am.
My voice lives within me.
It sounds within me
and without me
But never
without
me.

It sounds before me
and behind me
and where I am,
my voice
is.

My voice
moving through space
and time
becomes part of you.
The space of this room
bends my sounding voice back to me
as sound gives way
to silence...

My sonnet—or is it?

(from "Yes! Because...", first produced by Thunder's Mouth Theatre, Brisbane, 2015)

Most mornings, at the buzzing of my phone,
as magpies drink the early morning light,
I wake to find my flesh, my skin, my bones
reluctant to escape the dreaming night.

I like to be reminded, in good time
that I exist, that I am really here,
all present and correct in form and mind,
not just a shadow, or a figment in the rear

view mirror, speeding from the avalanche
of years expanding backwards, rear-
ending me into to the cavern
of shrunken years ahead that disappear

As fast as you look at them—

HAUD ON A MINNIT! 'at's no' a sonnet!
That's an angry old lady, ranting.

And I will rant and I will roar
and I will greet and roar some more

for I've been here before
and it was real—
and realising that—
is no big deal.

On writing poetry

I love a structure
so much better than a rupture.
It's divine, when there is time,
to tinker with a rhyme;

and to know that it's ok
to be imperfect, miss the boat
by a whisker, 'coz to play
is more important than the mote

in the eye of the beholder.
Stepping out and being bolder
than you were before—
that's what the game is for.

Structure keeps you safe while being brave—
and gives you the right to misbehave.

Villanelle: reminder to self

It's good to read, if you want to write,
to stretch the mind beyond its limitation.
Allow your eyes to let in more than light.

One idea, born in darkness, will take fright,
disguise itself, evade examination.
It's good to read, if you want to write.

That lone idea can't set itself alight
blundering around in frustration.
Allow your eyes to let in more than light.

To breathe in Inspiration is its right,
yet breath will not suffice for its gestation.
It's good to read, if you want to write.

To read is to encounter words in flight—
a murmuring of language in migration.
Allow your eyes to let in more than light.

When light and breath align to fuel your insight,
breathe deeply, have the courage to be erudite.
It's good to read, if you want to write—
allow your eyes to let in more than light.

A Tanka poem

Once bitten twice shy
there is no bitter outcry
your love bites softly
tastes my fearful loneliness
turns to seek out love elsewhere.

Fastest slug-slinger *in the (North) West*

A slug woke up today.
I am that slug.
I am that slug-a-bed,
iambic-ly I slug
my sluggish mounds of sliming flesh
into lively trochees
bouncing dactylic'lly down to the
kitchen to plug in the kettle and
knock up some breakfast, then—
anapaestic'lly make
up a reason to
be spon-da-ic-'lly a-wake.
Oh, too clever by half.
Not.

Uh-oh.
I'm doing that thing,

Slugging away,
slinging slugs at myself.
My son says I should
write about
other people
for a change.
He believes I can.
I believe he wants
another kind of mother—

one who doesn't just write
songs
          and poems
                    about herself.

He has a point though.

Apparently, the best comedians
use humour, aiming their slugs upwards
to knock those with power
from their perches.
That's what comedians do.
Speak truth to power.

I don't do that.
All my humour is self-deprecating.
I am the butt
of all my jokes.

And yet—some folk seem to relate to it.
Not because it gives them belly laughs.
Because it doesn't.
It's wry, it's gentle.
That doesn't mean it's not sharp.
I have the scars to prove it.

But then, I am not a comic.
I am not a comedian.
I am a clown.

It's my job to be a loser.

That's what clowns do.

It's their job to be in the doo-doo.

And I'm pretty good at that.

So there...

        I go...

                slugging away...

        slinging slugs at myself.

Money no object?

       Money no object, you say?
Alright then. Let's buy up shares
in big pharma, chuck out the CEOs,
hand over voting rights and control of the board
to small farmers, local doctors.
Let them choose the crops, the drugs
to be researched.

       Everything has its price.
Let's buy a few politicians. Check out their ancestry.
Promise we won't send them to
"detention" camps as long as they agree
to shut them down first.

       Any spare change?
Fill the homeless people's cups
brim-full with golden coins.
Stuff their pockets with
notes. Then turn away
and let them do with it
as they wish.

       Money can't buy love,
No. But giving it away is
a kind of love.

       I'd buy that.

Kindness matters

Kindness matters
in the night
walking home...

Where was I
when that act of kindness
struck me so deeply?
Walking home from an Open Mic
late one balmy night.
Popped into the last Tesco Express
about to close down so the staff
could get a few hours break.
Milk, I thought, almost run out.
Need milk in the morning.

I know I don't actually need milk
Can't possibly need it to sustain life.
There must be other ways to get calcium.
I'm not a baby—anymore.
Perhaps it stems from that time,
still war time,
my mother was travelling.
Who knows why she was travelling
with a 5 year old and a 3 month old baby?
Nevertheless, she was, and the baby was ill
crying, crying, crying,
unsightly boils on her head.

So the story goes.
They stopped at a hospital
in the middle of the night.
Emergency. I don't remember it, of course.
I was 3 months old
I may well have invented the
'middle of the night' part.
The diagnosis was malnutrition.
Why was that?
My mother wouldn't have deliberately
starved me, and although still war time
Australia didn't suffer from food restrictions.
Perhaps my mother was fed up
with the breast-feeding
Perhaps it was dried milk
that didn't suit me.

Perhaps my mother hadn't yet
realised that thing you discover
with the second child: that
what works for one baby
isn't necessarily right for another one.
I'll never know because
she wouldn't answer questions about 'the past'.
Obviously, I survived.

There I was, buying milk at midnight.
feeling conflicted about an encounter
earlier in the evening.

A new group of people who managed
to exclude me, although I doubt
they did it deliberately.
I hadn't made any great effort
to include myself
other than turning up.
So they either assumed
I wasn't interested in them
or that I was of no interest to them.

The evening wasn't a disaster though:
I left, headed to another event
where people I vaguely knew
welcomed me by name,
responded to my offerings
with enthusiasm.
Asked me to come back next time.

So where was I?
Leaving the late night supermarket
with my bottle of milk,
noticing the homeless dog
outside the door;
lifting my eyes to meet those of the
homeless man with the homeless dog.
I said "good night" as I passed him.
His voice, gently floating up the hill
touched my ears in the dark.
"Good night, my love."

So kind.
Such kindness in his voice.
I'm crying now as I remember it.

That's what kindness does.
It brings its own kind of pain,
It brings its own kind of pain
Infused with joy.

Kindness matters.

Ode to a butternut squash plant

O you lovely thing, sweetly savouring the
last receding flecks of late autumn sunshine
gently dancing, glancing on palest green leaves.
You cling with tendrils

thinly weaving round the wrought iron railing
that supported your greater need, your yearning
for fruition. Are you aware your days are
numbered? And do you

feel the loss of all the sweet babes you never
bore? One whole bright summer, that's all you had to
share the gift of life you were granted, only
one chance for you to

shine and show your flowers galore. And Bees came,
busy, buzzing, quivering, taking—something.
Leaving nothing useful behind, no gift for
you to create with.

Did you chide them? Did you complain? For you were
stunted, and constrained in a small black pot, no
kith or kin or neighbourly friendly roots to
share your own dreams with?

Sweetly, soaking sunshine and showers, imper-
ceptibly, expanding and curling, twisted
roots confined in plastic, an unforgiving
prison of false hopes.

As the weather turns and bright summer sunshine
fades to palest cool in the face of windy
storms, your blossoms fall in a heap of lemon
slips on the footpath.

Dreams have turned to dusty deliberations, to
thoughts of lost desires in the time we each have
left to dream.

Preamble to a song

The trip wasn't planned—
it was a diversion,
a blip in the timetable,
a visit to friends
not seen for a very long time;
to a treeless island,
flat but for three proud hills,
fringed with bright white sandy beaches,
frequented by—tormented by—
Atlantic gales.
Whose people are Gaelic speaking,
mild of manner and dry of wit.
The memories I had were sunken deeply
oceans ago and continents away
from love and loss.

And then, as the ferry turned
and chugged into the Sound,
the narrow strip of water
that rips the tide between two islands,
I began to re-cog-nise the landscape,
the gently undulating greenness,
the stone white houses
dotted here and there.
And I was overwhelmed with
the familiarity of it.
Remembering...

But not just remembering
what I already knew I remembered—
I was living it backwards
like the White Queen,
experiencing being alive
in the present moment of being there, then.

Yes, because now—there's a wind farm.
Does it count as a farm
if there's only one windmill?
Can you still call it a mill
if nothing is ground there
any more?
The old millhouse is a ruin
of tumbled stones,
fractured walls
whose crevices still ring
with the sound of the millhouse girls' giggles,
their mother's crackling call to come in!
Come inside, here's your tea, have a scone,
they're still warm.
And I cried...

I am old, Mother William, the lady cried
and she cried, and she cried.
And the windy sails turned
and her white head was burled
inside out, upside down
upside down, inside out.

Why return?
Asked the wind
and the sand and the tide.
I returned, Mother William
the lady replied,
I returned to be here.
I was here, I was here...

I am old, Mother William, the lady cried.
You were old yesterday,
sang the wind and the tide.
And the windy sails burned
and her old heart was turned
inside out, upside down
upside down, inside out.
I returned, Mother William,
the lady sighed.
I returned to be here
I was here
I am here...

with the wind
and the sand
and the tide.

An Episode

wherein I found myself, aged 70, in the best job in the world.

There I was, 39,999 feet above the Arabian Sea, one hour 33 minutes and 1,113 kilometres out from Dubai, vaguely noticing that the airline's information screen was, like me, still swivelling between Imperial and Metric, when it hit me. Really hit me. Even though I already knew it was happening, or I wouldn't be there in the first place.

I knew, in that 'oh my god really?' kind of way, in a 'what are they thinking do they have me confused with someone else' kind of way. But it had only been hovering around inside my head, teasing my neural pathways and occasionally spitting out of my mouth when people asked me about it. It hadn't dropped down into the core of my being, to that place where you feel things, a touch, a poke, a punch in the midriff that rocks you off balance—even though you are sitting down, strapped into a seat on an A380 Airbus 39,999 feet above the Arabian Sea.

How do they measure it? I wondered. From sea level? Does that mean from the top of the wave, or the bottom? The flight path information on the screen switched between 39,999 and 40,001. Maybe there were two foot waves down there. Up here it was all sunshine and air, tasteless scrambled eggs and weak coffee, great movies on a fuzzy screen, and no way to share this sudden shock of a reality check.

Dream Job. Someone asked me that a couple of days ago: "Is that your dream job?"

"Oh yes, I guess it is. Of course". But still it hadn't sunk in, and I still hadn't realised why such an expression exists. 'Sunk in'. Because that is exactly what it does. The mind catches a concept, the brain works its magic, converting it into actions that must be taken, like: book the flight, arrange for someone to look after the car, pack up and move out of the flat and into storage, get to the airport. And then, at some stage, if it is to work out at all well, it has to sink into the body and become part of the structure of every cell, a physical reality and not just a concept flickering across synapses.

I've been an actor long enough to know there is no mind/body separation. That is a conceptual illusion, articulated by Rene Descartes, misinterpreted and realigned over the centuries by philosophers and physical scientists creating school-of-thought empires for themselves, abused by politicians who will take advantage of any tool of divisiveness to keep their jobs. Actors, though, have to move beyond the purely conceptual as soon as they take the text that has been absorbed from the page out onto the floor. Words in the head do not resonate with an audience. They have to be voiced, and if all you are doing is speaking them aloud with nothing more than your understanding of their conceptual nature, you would do better to just hand out copies of the script to your audience, so they can read it, and conceptualise it for themselves.

So no. As an actor, you are obliged to translate the playwright's words into your own creative expression—without altering a syllable. And the words you express vocally are much more than mere concepts. They are the audible expression of your own lived, embodied, physically realised experience, even though the actual experience, in the context of the play, might be totally imaginary.

But I digress. And that's interesting too, to me at least. It occurs to me that no matter what I do, what I remember, what I experience, I will always digress into how that connects with acting. Sitting in that plane at 39,999 feet I had no idea just how much this job would teach me about ways of thinking about acting, ways of teaching acting and ultimately ways of acting.

So now, here I am, with less than four weeks to go before my contract is completed, trying very hard not to waste a single second of my remaining time here in regretting what else I could have done, or worrying about what might or might not happen after I leave. I've done my best to share as much knowledge and passion for voice training as I could with the actors-in-training who were entrusted to my care...

...and I still think this could turn into a book.

Where there's a pandemic

I'm ok—are you ok?

"How are you?" we ask each other.
"I'm ok".
Statement of fact.
"I'm ok..." Acknowledging
the absurdity of the question.
"I'm holding on!"
You don't need to do anything.
"It's a challenge, isn't it..."
We're in this together.

But then arrives the inevitable
"I'm struggling."

But you'll never hear me say that,
because as long as I am struggling—
please understand—
my struggle is
to challenge myself
to hold on
to being ok...
and then
I'll be ok.

How are you?

World on fire

World on fire,
and I am safely
marooned, larking about
with tattered remnants of
mythic tomfoolery,
weaving them into
the weft and warp of
fact versus fiction.

Not a good look for an undercooked clown,
not a bad look for an overlooked clown.
Searching for an escape route for a
deconstructed clown.

Music becalms my soul
torn from its moorings,
tossed across seas of unknown icy content.
Tears arouse fresh winds
to douse the flames
and I am safe again.
Within my cocoon my folded wings
resist the mould that teases and tempts them
to unhinge, to fly out into chaos.

No dicing with death.
Hold my breath, and play
in my own way.

Nobody sees me, no matter.
Still larking about, still looking in
To find the sacred space
wherein lies
motivation
to carry on
clowning.

The View from lockdown - I

10:04 am Tuesday 24th March, 2020. Not dead yet.

Decided to jot down what I've just been doing, so that I don't forget how industrious I can be if I try. And I suspect I will need to be industrious if I'm to stay sane in a pandemic world.

So, first thing, I made the bed. That's ok, eh? Got dressed, left my hair alone. No make-up, so must remember not to video myself today.

Checked on the garden, all good. Found that 'double daffodil' or is it a Jonquil? tipped over, so I pulled it and brought it in to play with its friends. It has the most exquisite, delicate perfume.

The perfume in the picture is Ralph Lauren Safari, which they don't make any more. I bought that bottle years ago on eBay, it was already well past its best, so now it has become an ornament.

I brought in from the 'garden shed'—a cupboard by the front door—the plastic bag I've been dumping stuff in ever since I moved here last May. Found some tiny bulbs, some of them rotten but others desperately sprouting pale and wan leaves, and I've popped them into a pot. I also re-potted the beautiful flowering plant that Sarah bought for me when she came to work on her audition monologue—she was accepted into the MA programme!

I listened dutifully to Radio 4 and the news, wondering when and if a State of Emergency, or Martial Law (whatever they call it here) will be declared, and having more sympathy than I ever thought I would for those nation states who have ever declared it, in this 'war' or any other. Who would have thought so many people would be so stupid as to travel from one infected country to another for a football match, or rush to the pub for yet another shouting match over a pint? Me. That's who.

Turned over to Radio 6Music and had a jolly good bop in the kitchen to Frankie Goes to Hollywood and Boney M. Now I'm tucking into my incredibly healthy breakfast, of muesli-with-extra-rolled-oats-and-almonds, a dash of milk and a topping of home-made yoghurt. I've made my second cup of coffee, and left it, forgotten, in the kitchen. The first one was left, forgotten, pouring all over the worktop because I'd left the machine on while I took stuff back to the garden shed. Hang on...

There it is. Lovely. Just needed a wee zap in the microwave. This one had been forgotten because my phone tinged, and it was a friend sending me a daft wee video on WhatApp. Janey Godley, Scots comedian, has taken a video of Nicola Sturgeon advising Scotland how to behave during the pandemic and added her own voice doing a creditable Nicola Sturgeon, only speaking in much broader Scots and making the message much more hilariously powerful.

I've forwarded it on to a few specially selected friends and my Scots born sons. I hate the mass sharings, when you know that the sender has just hit "send to all my contacts". I delete those immediately. Just so you know. Already, I've heard back from three of my actual friends, who've enjoyed the video and asked how I'm doing. That's what it's all about. Or should be.

Now I'm doing this, which has already exhausted its usefulness.

Catch you later. Stay at home. Wash your hands. Don't touch your face. (If you've been doing a lot of online communication lately, via Skype, FaceTime, Zoom, whatever, you're probably noticing, as I am, just how often we touch our faces.

Message to self: Don't do it. Even if you are socially distanced. It's an unconscious habit, and you'll do it when it's dangerous if you don't lose the habit.

A crack in the heart

Yesterday, a crack appeared in the heart.
The day before yesterday,
there was no cause for concern.
there was a strength in the beating pump
exchanging plasma for oxygen.

But yesterday, a crack appeared in the heart
and the pipes began to gurgle alarmingly
as sludge strained to refrain from
clogging up the plumbing for good.

Yesterday, a crack appeared in the heart.
And tears, not blood,
gushed and surged upwards!
Who knew that tears are stored down there
within that organ balanced oddly
between the lungs,
overseeing the distribution of life's
red river, lunging and retreating
while those twin tigers
Joy and Distress take turns at
lapping at its edges.

When a system fails, it reveals
processes hitherto concealed
within the comforting folds of
known scientific understanding.

Eyes do not see—
they receive. Brain does not know—
it sparks. Tears do not flow—
they leak. Hearts do not break—
they crack.
And sometimes they heal.
And sometimes, they erupt.

So now you know.

74

An X-istential poem

In an existential rabbit run
pandemic roller coaster fun
is likely to be overdone.
It's extraordinary
just how high the price is
when the oldest and quite possibly the wisest
are in exile from the youngest
who have exited their so-called education
to explore the other meaning of vacation.

Admit it! Sometimes
it's quite exciting,
examining our innermost extremities,
experimenting with external realities.
All in the face of
accelerating anomalies
revealing exacting complexities.

CoronaCoaster rap

Don't go out, they said.
Stay at home, keep your distance.
So what's new?
What's new is that it's not just me—
it's everybody!
I feel quite chuffed to be
part of a community.
All my life an oddity
refusing to conform
and now my way of life is—normal.
In years to come I'll fondly say:
those were the days,
finding novel ways
of keeping fear at bay,
tap dancing, baking,
anything pleasant,
having fun, guilt free.
This time was a Present!

And yet—there is no
pleasure without pain.
There are dips and dives
that yank my chain.
At first mini downward
spikes that come and go
without leaving a seaming
trail of destruction in their wake.

But sneakily they expand and slowly they grow
until they reach full strength and then they make
returning to the light a struggle
hardly worth the fight.

And then, I realise I still am not alone!
CoronaCoaster is the new name
for the new norm.
Hooray for normality!

Or not. Because time passes
or bends around us
depending on whether your glass is
half full, or overflowing.
And now our all-knowing
lords and masters
implore us to rearrange
our sequestered ways,
to fling our meagre savings
to the winds of All Change!
It's time to spend, spend, spend
the wages we don't have on
dining out and drinking up, and flying off.
"Four months this virus has been here
and I'm alright, so what's the problem?"
cry youthful voices,
believing it's their choice
to free themselves from the bondage
of behaving responsibly.

What price responsibility? Responsible
for whom? For children, whose lives
are never 'put on hold',
unless you tell them it is so.
Children continue to grow
to learn and play, to annoy each other
and their parents, day after day,
as children have done since
childhood was invented. Wherever they are,
school or home, their lives will be cemented
and augmented by the behaviour
of those who parent them.
Or responsible for the frail, the vulnerable, the old?
Who will surely die anyway. Sooner or later. Hello?

And so it goes. The pandemic engine
grunts and grinds and steams ahead
refusing to conform
before charging, with disrespectful
disregard, across the unsightly
wreckage of what we thought was normal.

Like time itself
CoronaCoaster has no reverse gear.
A sideways tilt disguised as a way out
is mere illusion, playing on our fears,
steering us deeper into temptation
to relax, sit back, and fall into a fallacy
A fantasy - a fakery.

We turn a corner, cheering for the sake of those
whose efforts appear to have applied the brakes,
diminished the danger, saved us from the monster
even as we realise the tracks ahead
are clearly zig-zagging
inexorably past countless points of no return.

If we look, if we gaze for long enough
we might see what lies in store.
I look, I gaze into the wide open door
of the warehouse within which is stored
my future, vaccine or no:
staying at home, keeping my distance,
coasting along through the rest of my life
with ups and downs and unexpected twists
and turns. So what's new?

What's new is this companion,
this CoronaCoaster
that is now a part of life itself.
At times I run beside it, then I ride it
up and down, side to side, never stopping,
no hopping off for a quick respite.
The new normal we fight for
will not be normal at all
until, inevitably, it becomes so.
Because unlike a roller coaster,
for a CoronaCoaster—
There Is No Going Back.

Two minutes silence and then what?

I stood in the kitchen and I wept.
No rejoicing in my heart
for the end of That War,
just despair at the lessons unlearnt,
the waste of life, of love, of potential:
the stupidity and apparently endless
regurgitation of sentimentality
with no responsibility—
I don't want to weep.

I want to rage from the rooftops
from the mountain tops
from the sky.
I want to scream
at the massed body of humanity
everyone who is, and whoever was:

"How can you be so stupid?
This is nothing new—
telling each other that
you are not alone? Of course not.
You are in the company
of every generation
that has ever experienced war,
famine, depression, plague, pandemics,
massed expulsions, forced emigration—
you were never alone.

Each generation perpetuates the lie,
the myth that somehow we can be different
we will never be so stupid as to allow ourselves
to go through that again.
And yet we are, and we do."

I don't do that, though.
I don't scream from the highest hill
because why wreck my voice by shouting
when I know nobody is listening?
not really listening.
Not even me.
I'm not listening, even to myself.
I only hear what I want to hear.
I am only human
and humans are inherently deaf to the message
they need to hear
if the species is to survive
even for a few more generations.

I don't worry about the planet.
Mother Earth will survive us
for as long as she is supposed to survive
given the nature of existence.
Species come and go,
mass extinctions
and mini extinctions will happen
in spite of humanity
and because of humanity.

Humanity will become extinct
because of itself.
We cannot blame an outside source,
we did it to ourselves.
End of story.

There is no going back.

Even if time existed in isolation
there is no going back.

There is only now
and now
and being
now
and then, now.

Standing in the kitchen,
Bent double with the force of the weeping
I still breathe.
I still think, feel, wonder
at the need to express all of this.
I know it will do no good.
Nothing will change
No life will be saved
by my actions
except, perhaps, mine.

The View from Lockdown - II

4:30 pm, Saturday 12th September. Still here.

What was I thinking, all those months ago, when I wrote "Day One of Journaling", saved the file in a folder on the desktop of my laptop, and then completely forgot all about it? It seemed like a good idea of the time? Story of my life.

Well, here I am at day two, six months later. I've been busy. Stuff has happened. And here we are again, on the verge of a badly needed, but poorly organised return to Lockdown. Never mind, I have no control over that.

What have I done today? I woke up, had a shower, took a pair of nail scissors to my very split ending hairs and snipped half an inch off all round—sort of.

Downstairs, I was struck by the brightness of the light—so welcome after many days of mostly grey skies. The birds have only eaten half of the seeds I put out for them last night. After months of glorious birdsong, we are now back down to a pair of wood pigeons and the usual seagulls. Lockdown came at the best time of the year, early spring, so the absence of road and air traffic provided space, in sound and sight, for the birds to fill. But I digress. This is supposed to be about today. While getting dressed, I listened to a chapter or so of Carlo Rovelli reading his book *Seven Brief Lessons on Physics*[1].

---

[1] *Seven Brief Lessons on Physics,* Carlo Rovelli. Penguin 2016.

What a joy! I don't expect to come to the end of it as an expert physicist, on the contrary I reckon I only understand about one percent of what he is saying, but I treasure that one percent.

I don't buy the idea that particles of matter only exist when they are being observed. For pedantic me, (because language is important) it makes more sense to say that they are only available to be observed if we pay attention to them.

"Everything that exists is never stable, and is nothing but a jump from one interaction to another", says Mr Rovelli. Aha! say I, that is also the case with human relationships. He compares Newton's mechanical world (with its immutable certainties) with the Quantum world of "continuous, restless forming of things—a continuous coming to light and disappearance of ephemeral entities". A world of happenings, not of things. That makes my brain feel happy.

I am reminded of the first academic essay I ever wrote, "Voice as Event/s", presented at my first conference and consequently published in the Melbourne post-graduate journal AntiTHESIS. Ah, those were the heady days, when I first discovered how philosophical theories could inform my practice as a performer. My long-suffering acting students were subjected to a new one every week, as I encountered each new school of thought.

Rovelli's words also set my thoughts on a process of creating an analogy. There are tens of thousands of individuals around the world, whose conviction that a Covid-19-free-life is possible-if-they-pretend-the-virus-doesn't-exist, is dependent on a Newtonian world of immutable certainties; and then there are the rest of us, condemned to function in a highly unstable, mutable and increasingly ephemeral (or quantum) way of life. Perhaps those others are right, and if so we will just die out, leaving only those with an inbuilt immunity to carry on destroying the planet.

Meantime, I had breakfast. More homemade yoghurt, and a slice of toast and marmalade. (Six months' practice has improved the quality of both my yoghurt and bread-making, thank goodness!) A stroll round my so-called garden. Why do I denigrate my garden? It is a garden, just not like any other.

My garden is a bunch of plants in pots spread around the paved yard outside my house. It's wild and wacky, not by plan but by nature. Here is how it works: I plan what goes into the pots, be it tomato plants, a rose bush, small fruit trees, or parsley or lemon geraniums for example, and nature throws up pansies, snapdragons and monkey-face flowers around them. Who knew that would be possible? Certainly not me.

Being an elderly person, I am shielding for the duration of the pandemic, and my garden keeps me supplied with salad and vegetable greens, tomatoes and flowers, fresh air and peace. I can't imagine how I would have survived thus far if I had still be living in my second floor studio flat in the city centre during this time.

Back to journaling... Oh yes, and I sorted out my set list for a Zoom folk club session I'll be taking part in next Tuesday. A wee rehearsal, checking on my accent for a Scots folk song and learning the new verse I've added to one of my originals. So far, so lunchtime.

After lunch it was back to the computer, checking to see if there were any stray poems hanging around in odd files that I could turn into a new song. And hey presto! I found this file. So there you have it. My life in Lockdown, in two episodes. And it's not over yet. See you in another six months.

Song of the crone

Another day
like yesterday,
a bit of work
perhaps some play.
What to do?
What to say?
Not quite here
nor a mile away.

What to do?
No.
What to do!
There is always
something to do.
To do, or not to do?
Nothing to say but—
what to do!

When I have done
what I have to do
will there be something
else to do?
So far, it's not a great to-do,
I've always found
something else to do.
Round I go
doing and doing,

time spent wisely
or doing undoing.
You cannot go back
but you can unpick
and that is a doing
of re-construing,
whatever was done,
making a-new-ing.

When I have done
what I was doing,
fail or succeed
I'll always need
to do whatever
I want to do
as soon as I can.
Jumping to fire
from frying pan.
No time to waste.
It's the Song of the Crone
"Is that for me?
Can I do that too?
I know I can make it my own."
So much to do
so little time.
All it needs
is a taste for rhyme.

Not a word of a lie

What to say?
Who to say it to?
Why say it?
When to say it?
Where...?
Oh yes. That's right.
There is no where there.
It's all here, dear.
The message is clear, dear.
Where you are is there, now.
Well then - When?
I asked that before
I guess the raven understood the score
Because if not now, or even then,
All that's left is Never More.

There is a thread
A fine and fragile thread
That holds my heart,
That winds around my heart
Connects it to a chamber in my skull.
In my heart, there is a chamber,
A sweet room with walls of softness.

There was a moment when I thought,
"This could go on forever!"

And then I thought I'd cry
And then I thought—
What difference would that make?
So I didn't do that.

Who said what, and why wouldn't you?
Has anything been done about it?
What can't I be doing with this?
Let the sky fall. Let the rain fall.
Let's call out the rain.
Downhill all the way.

Is this too fast for you?
Too many questions?
Never stop asking questions.
When you don't ask questions
It's because you think you know
All the answers.

I could write a book at this rate
Full of nothing. THE Book of Nothing.
I'd call it "Post-apocalyptic Me:
A Creation Myth at the End of the Rainbow."

The window is weeping
tears not rain
sweeping down
drowning out
the words we spoke before.

The wind is sweeping
clutching leaves
that cannot fall
but hold on fast
to what they had before.

The dark is creeping
slowly draining
hope and patience,
grace, forbearance,
values held before.

The sun is peeping
up above
beyond the clouds
that clear away
the myth that was before.

The future's keeping
all our dreams
of better days,

to give us time
to leave what was before.

This Time is reaping
what we sowed
and now we owe it
to ourselves
to own what went before.

The earth's house-keeping
bill is due,
payment in lieu
will not do what it
might have done before.

The day is sleeping
calmy breathing
through the storm
waiting for
whatever lies in store.

Song Lyrics

Autobiography

(from "The View from Over the Hill" touring post pandemic...)

I was born in Australia,
my mother was a dressmaker,
my father was a sailor.
I dreamt of being an actor,
but was terrified of failure—
what's more, I didn't fit in,
so I packed my paraphernalia,

and I did what all young Aussies did,
took a trip on a great big ship,
headed for London town.
But instead of becoming a West End Star
I got married and settled down—

with a Scottish folk singer,
who got me to sing "The Drover's Dream"
over and over and over again...
Then we opened a restaurant, on a remote
Scottish Isle in the Hebrides, accessible by boat—
unless the Atlantic winds blew up a storm
I soon discovered that was just the norm.
So we went bust, and had to shift
with our two little boys, till we could lift
our finances out of the ditch—
four years in Nigeria did the trick.

Back in Scotland, our boys were growing up fast,
their teenage years soon passed.
I played the Fringe, I taught and I toured,
my acting ambitions still endured
so in an attempt to get myself cured...

I went back to Australia in 1996,
discovered it still wasn't my bailiwick.
Now I'm here in England, and I'm here to stay,
it'll take more than a points system to drive me away.
I still teach and tour and I play the fringe,
my daft little songs are my repertoire,
and if, at my age, that seems unhinged
it is my life, so far.
 Still not a West End Star.

My two little boys are now grown men
there are three grandkids, two grand dogs
and two grand kittens.
And none of us lives in Australia
but Zoom is the great communication enable-ier!
So not a complete failure!

Pre-breakfast blues

*(from the play "One Point Five" produced by The Wicked Ladies,
Glasgow 1989, and revised as "Blame it On Your Mother" by Les Girls,
Toowoomba 2003)*

I woke up this morning
with nothing in my mind—
nothing but a half remembered dream.
It only takes a moment
for the world to flood on in,
a moment in a lifetime
a ripple in a stream.

*I've got those pre-breakfast blues.
Oh Lordy let me snooze.
Take me back to the land of dreams
where there's nothing to lose.*

No sense of blame or shame
lit up my sleep befuddled brain.
I did have hungry kids to feed,
a house to clean, a garden to weed,
clothes to wash and iron and mend
and oh, my lord! When would it end?

There's no life like a housewife's
for low job satisfaction.
I'm ripe for the good life
with intellectual interaction...
Mmmmmmm—Uh-oh! I wonder if he heard?

Could my thoughts have penetrated his dreams?
It only takes a moment for the world to flood in
and in that moment wash away
the best laid schemes.

Why am I sympathising with a man who's fast asleep?
I've got the dreams while
he's got the schemes and—he can keep them.

Pre-breakfast blues.
Oh Lordy let me snooze.
Take me back to the land of dreams
Where there's nothing to lose.

The kids are up, they're getting dressed,
they don't need me at all.
They can wash and clothe and feed themselves too.
It only takes a moment to change from child to man.
One moment you're a mother, the next an also-ran.

Oh! pre-breakfast blues.
Oh Lordy let me snooze.
Take me back to the land of dreams
Where there's nothing to lose.

When I woke up this morning,
I'd nothing on my mind—
just an empty space, where I can place a dream.

Blame it on your mother

(from "One Point Five" and "Blame it On Your Mother")

Are your eyes blue or green?
Are your teeth squeaky clean?
Do you walk with a dash or a hobble?
Are you short, fat or thin?
Are you ugly as sin?
Do your curvy bits curve, or just wobble?

Do you wake up each morning
as bright as the lark?
Or grouse through the day
like a plover?
Don't be afraid
it's the way that SHE made you—
blame it on your mother.

You can't help but follow on
the way your mother always led;
she showed you how to clean a house
and keep your family fed.

So if you can't quite do it right
there's nothing to be said.
Coz mother knew
what's best for you,
she said you were a slut
and you know it's true...

My mother told me, I never shouldie
play with the boys in the magic woodie
How could she know that I ever couldie
turn out the way that she knew I wouldie?

Are you sharp as a nail
or as dull as a snail?
Do you sing like a bird, flat or sharp-o?
Do you like your men tall
or straight off the wall,
take your Marx, let it be Karl, or Harpo.

Are your kids always neat
or the shame of the street?
Can you say, hand on heart
"They're no bother!"

If they're out of control,
there won't be a soul who won't
blame it on their Mother—
         That's you!
Coz you love them like no other
         I told you
you just take after your mother!

Like you do

(from"Yes! Because...", produced by Thunder's Mouth Theatre,
Brisbane, 2015)

Trees are green, or so they seem,
skies are blue, it's what they do.
Roads are grey, they fade away
        like you do.

Days are long, but I drive on,
in a bridge or two I'll be over you.
Some starry night I'll see the light
        right through you.

I'm heading over the range, down to the plain
I'll find a bus or a boat or a train
to take me some place where nobody knows me
        like you do.

Nights are black, and there's no turning back.
Come the dawn I'll be long gone.
I've time to kill and I won't stand still
        like you do.

I'm heading over the hills, down to the sea.
There'll be a job just waiting for me
and people who like to do things that I like,
        not like you do.

Nights are still black, there's no turning back.
Come the dawn I'll be long gone.
It might take a while to find my style.
If I stuff up I'll just knock back the cup
  (Me and Socrates!)
There'll be no commotion as I drink the potion
that is my special brew.
I'll finally learn to face life on my own terms
(you got it -)
  like you do.

Dreams of handsome men

(from "Yes! Because...")

I have dreams of handsome men
behind my eyes, beneath my pen.
each one wise enough to know
that dreaming is the only way to go.

So I take them to those places in my heart,
places where I dare not go alone,
and only when their handsome faces fall apart
can I return to find my fears are gone.

I am wise beyond my years
after wine, amongst my peers.
Courage in another's strife is much
more potent, and less lonely
when it's Dutch.

I'm giving up the blues, what have I got to lose
but my heart?
Drop the guard, let music take control.
The heart will beat more soundly,
be more whole.

I've been told I'll never have
a love to match the love I give.
If I thought that were so
I'd settle here and now
for any love that's going anyhow.

But I have dreams of handsome men
behind my eyes, beneath my pen.
Each one wise enough to know
that dreaming is the only—
don't you tell me I'm lonely—
dreaming is the only way to go.

*(Winner of Open Section, Gold Coast Poetry Competition
1997)*

Lament of the 6 year old

(from "Blame it On Your Mother" and "Yes! Because...")

I wish I were adopted almost every day,
then my real live mother
would come 'n' take me away.
She'd love me and she'd care for me
she'd read to me each night,
she'd let me sleep till lunchtime and
she'd never turn out the light.

Oh! I'm telling you, something's very wrong
I shouldn't be here, I do not belong.
This family is really weird,
they kidnapped me at birth.
Coz I'm the child of the totally wild
Queen of Middle Earth.

I'm sure I was adopted, I heard my mother say
she never wanted children, they just get in the way.
She tries to lie and tell me that "I'm so glad I have you"
She's quite a clever actress, but I know it's not true.

I know I was adopted, I feel it in my bones.
My mother really hates me, she never leaves me alone;
she talks to all my teachers and she believes it's true
that homework and broccoli are really good for you.

Oh! I'm telling you, something's very wrong.
I shouldn't be here, I do not belong.

This family is really weird,
they kidnapped me at birth.
Coz I'm the child of the totally wild
Queen of Middle Earth.

I feel that I'm adopted, almost all the time.
I think I'll have to run away, it would be sublime
to find my proper mother, who'd always let me play
with water, and with matches and in the drive-way!

I'm sure that I'm adopted,
it has to be the truth.
My fake mum's really ruthless,
while I'm just FULL of ruth.
My real mum's on her way here,
I'm sure it won't be long—
in fact, she's coming through that door
before I finish this song [PAUSE]

Oh, I'm telling you, something's very wrong.
I shouldn't be here, I do not belong.
This family is really weird,
they kidnapped me at birth.
Coz I'm the fairest,
long lost dearest
sweet and cuddly
cute and lovely
I'm the child of the totally wild
Queen of Middle Earth.

Wallflower song

(from "Yes! Because...")

Do you see me? Am I really here?
Can you hear me? Could I be more clear?
If you touched me, would I survive?
How can I thrive when my skin is so alive?

Could you want me? What a question's that?
Would you taunt me if I turned my back?
Hoping, dreading, longing for the chance
to find out what the books mean
when they speak of romance.

When will it be my turn to dance the night away
with a boy who isn't pimply,
a boy who isn't gay?
I want a boy, but not any boy will do.
It must be a boy who looks... like...

You don't see me. I'm not really here.
I can't hear you—my ears are full of fear.
You are walking up to me to ask me for the name
of the girl who stands and twirls into your
arms and I will learn again that—

You don't see me, I'm not really here
You can't hear me, even though I'm near
So I will go my own way—and I will learn at last, that
I can dance to my own tune, until the moment's passed.

Greatest giver-upper in the world

(from "Yes! Because...")

I am the greatest giver-upper in the world
When it comes to resignation
I claim the designation.
I've given up on diets
I've given up on men
I've even given up on myself—
now and then!

I gave up on sport,
the other kids were just too rough,
I gave up on ballet,
my legs weren't long enough.
I gave up on piano
when they took my prize away,
and I gave up tap dancing—
I couldn't make it pay.

Oh yes, I am the greatest giver-upper in the world.
If there's defeat around,
I'll take it, lying down.
Of losers I'm the queen
I'm the best that's ever been
and if you don't believe me
I'll show you what I mean...

I gave up on yoga,
couldn't hold a pose for long.
I gave up doing weights,
my muscles don't like being strong!
When jogging was in fashion
my knees couldn't take the strain.
And I gave up bike riding—
falling off just causes pain.

Oh yes, I am the greatest giver-upper in the world
My failure rate's so high
eagles cheer as it flies by.
And I don't know how to stop
being such a stunning flop
so I guess I'll keep on giving up
until the day I drop.

I gave up writing plays—
no one wants to see 'em.
My characters are so far-fetched
no one want to be 'em.
I gave up singing opera—
my high notes would crack your specs!
And I gave up singing jazz
coz my low notes were too sexy...

Oh yes, I am the greatest giver-upper in the world.
If there's defeat around
I'll take it, lying down.

Of losers I'm the queen,
I'm the best that's ever been,
and if you don't believe me
I will show you what I mean—

Except I've given that up too.

The Fairy Queen rap

(from "Yes! Because...")

They said I was too old to play the Fairy Queen,
which heralded the end of my
Midsummer's Dreammm-ming...
But I staggered on, to spite them, for a time,
playing Fairies in the Christmas Pantomime.

I loved the sequined frocks—
not so much the stiletto heels,
or the poison-belching fog machine,
the trap door that shot you on stage between
the lover's tryst and the comics' routine—
and I loved the Act Three reveals.

And I'd do it again in a heartbeat
I'd dress up and make up and start leap
-ing round and around and around
and around and around
until I get dizzy and then I'd fall down..
(Here we go!)
And let's face it, no-one wants an ancient fairy—
at least not the kind I could play.
What with senility impending,
knees and hips in need of mending,
I should get with the times
and put all my rhymes
To good use, in the most modern way.

Coz it's all rap now, isn't it?
Well, how hard can it be?

No-one wants an ancient fairy,
not even if she's really hairy,
'coz that would just be scary,
and even contrary,
'coz a fairy with a beard—
well that's just weird.
It isn't cute to be hirsute.
That is not an attribute
that I would recommend
to a friend
on Facebook.

Like the Wily Wicked Wizard
who's still on my casebook...

Yes no-one wants a fairy that's oldie
'coz she will just be mouldy and coldie,
and her joints will ache
and she'll maybe break
her hip, so she can't hop, and that's not hip.
No, 'coz it's a rule
that fairies should be cool
not twerky, like Mylie
but quirky, more like Kylie
(She might be getting on,
but she's no turkey!)

So! a fairy don't need to be flex—
she don't need a reason.
She can still want sex—
she don't need a reason,
'coz she still got magic.
No, she ain't tragic,
she don't need gadgets
or even Plantagenets
to Fly Around the World!

To my mother

(from "Blame it On Your Mother" and "Yes! Because...")

When I was young I wondered why
you hid yourself from me.
I tried to find the woman
your friends thought you to be.
They'd tell me how you made them laugh
and they made you laugh too—
I thought they must be kidding.
It didn't sound like you.

To me you seemed remote and cool,
you never cared to touch.
So when I went away to school
I didn't mind so much.
You let me go so easily, and
I thought "I don't mind"
Why should I? It's just another
place I leave behind."

So I left home determined
to never be like you.
I'd laugh and play with my kids
I'd kiss and hug them too.
But I found myself repeating things
that you had said to me.
I tried to say them kindly.

I tried to let them be
the best that they can be,
not stunted, the way I seemed to be.

And then at last I grew up and found
I could let you go.
I'm proud to be the woman
that you have come to know.
I found that I could make you laugh
and you made me laugh too.
You took the time to find me, and
I'm
glad
I
found
you.

Ina Hofmaster 1915 - 2017

Singer of songs (teller of tales)

Here comes a singer of songs,
songs to make you laugh away the dust of day,
    the must of clay.
She'll bring you joy for all the springs
    that autumn never knew,
the dew upon the meadows where the
    sunset never grew
the magic of an opal flashing blue—blue—blue—
    she'll bring you songs,
    she'll sing of wonder.

Do you wonder why a sorrow
never shared is never lost?
The fingers of the clock hands linger,
clutching, and reaching,
scratching scars that
touch your soul with frost—
    for time is now,
    or time is never

Here's a teller of tales,
tales to make you weep for all the pain of man,
    the final plan.
He'll give you Ceres weeping
    in the cancer of her prime,
the children of the famine
    and the victims of our crime,

the madness and the sadness
            and the badness of our time,
      he'll tell you tales,
      he'll tell of wonder.

Do you wonder why the day is longer
than the day is true?
Why it turns the night
within its tightness
holding, and moulding,
scolding Life and forcing it anew,
      for life is now
      or life is never.

Here comes a poet with rhymes,
rhymes to make us think about the things we say,
      the games we play.
She'll drum your heart with stranger beats
      that stir you from within,
a turn of phrase will catch your breath then
      let it flow again.
The words will split your mind apart
            and set it in a spin,
      she'll bring you rhymes,
      she'll make you wonder.

Do you wonder why the more we know
the less we understand? How
ignorance can spread like wildfire,

needing, and bleeding,
feeding on our greed and lack of grace,
        for grace is now
        or grace is never.

Here come the singers of songs,
songs to make you laugh away the rust of day,
        it's just the way
of singers since the earth was new
        and songs were there to sing,
since man discovered woman
        and enslaved her with a ring,
since laughter fed on sorrow, prince or
                peasant, clown or king,
        we'll bring you songs
        we'll sing of wonder.

Attilla of Tails—Tale-Tailer
*(Thoughts while walking, talking to Siri, who couldn't
handle the phrases "a teller of tales, tale-teller")*
I am Attilla, the tale-teller,
I tailor tales in verse and song,
my verse as predictable as the day is long.
But days can be short
and predictions can be wrong.
I bring you tales—I bring you
tales of longeur.

About the Author

Anton Mellor Photography

Flloyd Kennedy, Liverpool-based, Australian-born actor, singer-songwriter, performance poet, director and voice/speech/accent coach, took part in the British folk revival in the late 1960s, performed street theatre, cabaret and fringe theatre in Scotland throughout the 1980s and 90s, established Golden Age Theatre to tour contemporary and classic theatre throughout Scotland. She returned to Australia in 1997 where she undertook research into the performing voice (specifically Shakespeare) for her doctorate. Flloyd teaches voice and acting skills at colleges and universities in the UK, US and Australia, currently teaching online through her private studio Being in Voice and regularly performs at online Open Mic spoken word and music events. In non-pandemic times she tours her solo verse plays with music around the world. She has two sons, three grandchildren, two grand dogs and two grand kittens, and is a proud member of Equity.

Acknowledgements

I would like to thank Anke McLean for taking the care in these troubled times to read the draft MS and to comment and encourage me so thoroughly, Martin Williams for his excellent and rigorous proof reading, and Terry Cripps for the beautiful and intriguing cover design. Also thanks to all the kind friends, family and colleagues who have chivvied me on over many years to perform and to publish my work.

Also by Flloyd Kennedy
BOOKS

Sunsets & Kites

scatterings of light and dark in poems, songs and essays

"funny, wonderfully anarchic and bonkers" *Jane Vicary*

"the real deal: honest, unsparing, hilarious and heartfelt. Her wryly observed stories, told in poetry and song" *Lauren Grodstein*

"Flloyd's book is a blockbuster, get in there for a nice present or something to cuddle up with these dark winter months" *George Melling*

"I found all the poems and stories entertaining and thought provoking, and some of them I'll go back and read again - and possibly again!" *Mabel Macarthur*

"There is a slowness in this book that is missing in the world. A kindness. A gentle beauty to the words and rhythms that allows the deeper meanings to move in the shadows" *Ted Gray*

(available in paperback, eBook and audiobook)

Shish Mahal Cook Book

compiled by Flloyd Kennedy

Alloway Publishing, Ayr 1982

all proceeds to the Prince & Princes of Wales Hospice, Glasgow.

"A lovely little gem. I've tried a few recipes from this book with gr8 success. The chicken dhansak is very tasty but to be fair they all nice. I would recommend this book whatever your ability is on the curry ladder."

"Fantastic recipes, who would have thought those delicious onions you get with your pappadums are marinated in ketchup! Best Indian recipe book ever (and I do have other Indian cookbooks now)."

"The book is very informative and the recipes are excellent every time. Brings back great memories of when the "shish" was just a one room restaurant. In Gibson Street Glasgow."

MUSIC

The songs are available online as singles from

Bandcamp

https://flloydwith2ells.bandcamp.com/

also Spotify, Apple Music, Google Play, Amazon Music

and all major music streaming sites.

Songs from "Yes! Because..."

CD available from flloyd@flloydkennedy.com

£5 plus postage and packaging

Quote code AFTERSUNSET